Poems of Life

by

Paul Fronda

First published in the United Kingdom in 2014
by Paul Fronda

Copyright © Paul Fronda 2014

ISBN 978 0 9930132 2 5

Printed by Hobbs the Printers Ltd
Totton, Hampshire SO40 3WX
www.hobbs.uk.com

CONTENTS

A lifting thought, an encouraging word,
When they come from God they are truly heard.
Open your heart, draw closer to him.
Let His anointed words come forth
and find their home within.
When they reach the heart of the willing soul,
It is then they are written for God's glory to be told.

THE
JOURNEY

THE WALK OF LIFE

With "Goo" and "Gah"—
The first crawl that doesn't get far.

Those wobbly walks
and the excitement of talk.

The time of going through school—
Not ending up a fool.

A time of work and rest,
a time of doing our best ...

... to improve our life
with those things nice.

Now a time to retire
before we die—
The walk of life has
Just passed you by.

But to start again
without life's pain...

A life without strife,
with everything nice.

With joy and peace,
living life's feast.

But, end of the day,
man has his say.

His choice to choose:
Win or lose.

To laugh or cry
before his last sigh.

The walk of life
has just passed you by.

THE TUG OF GOD'S HAND

What more could I ask? What more could I receive?
But to walk this life, just Jesus and me.

He holds my hand wherever I go.
He tells me things that I should know.

To be in his presence is an overwhelming place,
with his endless love and amazing grace.

Every new day that comes is a day to shine,
just to hold His hand and know all is fine.

I know my time here with him one day will end,
but until such time, I hold the hand of my friend.

And when that day comes, I shall understand,
as I feel that gentle tug of God's hand.

NEXT PLEASE

Circling around the mighty throne
Is all I know as my home.
Waiting and waiting with so much intent
for a chance to be sent.
To experience a thing that's called 'life'.
They tell me it's supposed to be very nice.
Someone says, "He made His choice."
Then next I hear His mighty voice,
"NEXT PLEASE!"

Nine months of darkness has comforted me,
But now at last I'm set free.
I look around; there's no-one I know
but a reassuring voice say's, "Hello."
A new voice has entered my brain.
Someone has just given me a new name.
"NEXT PLEASE!"

They say I have to go to school!
Or I'll end up being a fool.
This time of my life seems so slow.
Some days I don't want to go.
The time at last has filled my brain
And now I hear them call my name.
"NEXT PLEASE!"

From school to the jobless queue of despair
Those in front don't even care.
I'm told there's a job waiting for me.
But only a glimmer of hope I see.
Week after week is still the same,
Until at last they call my name.
"NEXT PLEASE!"

They say to enjoy work you have to be keen
with 9-5 as the routine.
Bed, work, home, bed—Is this all that can be said
For all those years that lie ahead?
This part of life is the hardest yet
But it won't be long till I can forget.
For round the corner, not long to be
Is retirement time, waiting for me.
But I know things won't be the same
as somebody calls out my name.
"NEXT PLEASE!"

Afternoon naps, afternoon teas,
glasses on the end of my nose to help me read.
Stiff joints, walking stick,
Help me to the doctor's when I'm sick.
Pill after pill all I take
But at my age it's far to late.
They say I'm off to a place of rest,

But with a moan I soon protest.
All around me are people in chairs
Those who don't sleep just gaze in the air.
Memories and forgetful minds,
Trying to capture all lost time.
All the things I wish I had done,
Those lost chances of having fun.
But now around me is what is left for me:
a piece of cake and a cup of tea.
Heavy eyelids and a deep down sigh,
I close my eyes and say goodbye.
And once again a voice calls my name:
"NEXT PLEASE!"

Darkness, darkness, all around me;
I'm on a journey but cannot see.
People are crying and saying nice things.
People around me are trying to sing.
Someone calls my name from above;
All I can feel is so much love!
Then somebody takes me by the hand
And says we are going home to a better land.
On my way to my new home
I look down to see
What is written on my stone
"NEXT PLEASE!"

A TRUE FRIEND

An encouraging true friend is God's blessing.
Their timely words are always refreshing.

Such a friend is there with an open ear
to listen to any doubts or fears.

They are always there with an arm to lend,
with comforting words to help you mend.

That phone call any time—night or day,
they always welcome what you have to say.

They say a true friend is closer than a brother.
How true that is when in the presence of each other.

A period of time may keep you apart,
but that special true friend will never depart.

Some people go through life and a true friend never find,
but a God-sent true friend is one of a kind.

THE CLOCK

Tick-tock, tick-tock goes
life's endless clock.
Sometimes fast, sometimes slow,
where we end up, only time will show.

Tick-tock, tick tock goes
life's endless clock.
For seasons come and seasons go.
No sooner the sun than back to snow.

Tick-tock, tick tock goes
life's endless clock.
Searching and searching for knowledge untold,
a million miles from things of old.

Tick-tock, tick tock goes
life's endless clock.
Ever seeking, ever perceiving,
but always searching for a reason.

Tick-tock, tick tock goes
life's endless clock.
For man in his wisdom thinks he knows it all,
but, compared to his maker, he's only a fool.

Tick-tock, tick tock goes
life's endless clock.
For who knows what is good for man
during his few and meaningless days?
He passes through like a shadow
and fades away in the shade.

Tick-tock, tick tock goes
life's endless clock.

GOD'S RHYTHM OF LIFE

What is this sound I hear in the night?
It seems to appear when everything is quiet.

A rhythm of sound that doesn't miss a beat.
I look out of the window, "Is it coming from the street."

But the street is all quiet, and there's nothing to show.
Where it's coming from I just don't know.

The morning comes, and the sound disappears.
All I can hear now is worldly chatter in my ears.

The nights come around, and I listen to the same old sound,
Seeking answers to this mystery that need to be found.

Now there's new life in the family, and I am there at hand;
a visit to the hospital to see this life with a scan.

A knob is turned, a sound I hear
A heartbeat of life I hear with my ears.

But wait! It's the same sound I hear in the night.
At last! I have the answer that I know now is right.

Oh what a day, it has turned out so nice!
The mystery of the sound: Is God's Rhythm of Life.

ADVERSITY

WHEN THINGS GET TOUGH

When things get tough and don't go your way,
when you've done all you know to do,
keep standing strong and pray.

Keep us steadfast in faith,
under the shadow of your wings,
until the storms pass; and, by your grace,
await for the new day you bring.

For when the storms come,
we sometimes bend like a reed,
but you, Lord, our strong deliverer,
are there in our time of need.

And with new strength we shall rise up like the eagle
and soar once again.
In glorious victory with you, we will always reign.

Keep believing, keep singing songs of praise.
Keep fighting the good fight –
God's promise of victory is on its way.

Sometimes problems mean life isn't a ball
but one thing's for sure:
The Lord will deliver us from them all.

THEY BOW

As we walk along life's road,
We face problems that don't seem to go.

Where there was one, now there are many.
There was a time when there weren't any.

We take control, and we pray all night,
But those problems just put up a fight.

Overwhelmingly they come, and come on strong.
If only we could put them where they belong.

Where's our faith? Where's our belief?
We know it's what we need for relief.

Then the light turns on, thank God at last –
Now we can put those problems in the past!

So, in Jesus name, we command them to go.
One by one they bow, gone with nothing to show.

YOUR NEW LIFE

The devil's grip on your life cannot remain
When you stand in faith in Jesus' name.

All bondage is broken over your life;
Satan's schemes destroyed, there's no more strife.

God is getting ready to put an end to your pain.
Your endless toil will no longer remain.

Every mountain in your life will be made low;
The crooked paths made straight as you go.

God has a plan for you—He says, "Call to me!
I will show you things you do not see."

He wants to show you great and mighty things;
His overflowing favour He will bring.

He's the healer, the restorer of everything;
So rise up, worship Him, and see your new life begin!

THE STRUGGLE

Why am I struggling, Lord,
with all the things I do?
It shouldn't be like this, Lord,
when I belong to you.

Is the reason my stubborn pride –
that these struggles surround me?
If I were to humble myself,
would it set me free?

Or maybe, Lord, I'm far away
from your guiding ways,
making me disobedient
to the words you say.

If I say I'm sorry, Lord,
for all the things I've done,
would it turn these struggles
into a life of fun?

Lord, am I doing something wrong?
Is there anything I should know?
If you were to tell me, Lord,
these struggles would surely go.

A KNOCK AT THE DOOR

Trouble has come knocking at my door,
with words of 'Why, Lord?'
I haven't broken any law.

This time of trouble has found me.
Show me a way out, Lord,
that I might see.

As I wait and trust in Him,
impatience arises from within.

Now would be good, Lord,
Now's a good time!
A little attention please, would be fine.

Still I wait,
I wait in vain.
A voice of desperation I try to contain.

Who do I turn to,
If not you?
A little sign, Lord, to see me through.

Still no answer, still no sign.
Then a voice within says,
'All will be fine.'

Have faith in me,
Faith from your heart.
I will make this trouble depart.

A new knock at the door.
I open wide.
'Come in peace. Come inside!'

GOOD SOUND ADVICE

Amidst all of the rows and all the shouts
and all of life's troubles
and all those nagging doubts . . .

there's a place called peace, a place to be.
Take the hand of Jesus,
and He will set you free.

With no more strife and no more tears,
when you walk with Jesus
there are no more fears.

When times are tough, when they come at you,
Jesus is always there
to get you through.

The choice is yours—how you live your life.
But knowing Jesus
is Good Sound Advice.

WITH YOU I GET THROUGH

Light of my life, I'm so glad I have you.
In all of life's troubles, with you I get through.

Walking life's road, with you arm in arm,
one word from you—and the storms are calm.

And even the times when I might fall,
faithful and forgiving, you're there when I call.

And then there are times when I might roam,
but you're always there to guide me home.

What more could I ask for, what more could I say?
With your loving presence, I face a new day.

Light of my life, I'm so glad I have you.
In all of life's troubles, with you I get through.

WHEN YOU SET YOUR EYES ON JESUS

No matter how bad things appear to be,
when you set your eyes on Jesus,
He will set you free.

As our earthly reasons all run dry,
when you set your eyes on Jesus
There'll be no more need to sigh.

And, faced with problems to be solved,
when you set your eyes on Jesus,
He will get involved.

It doesn't matter—problems big or small,
when you set your eyes on Jesus,
He's there for you to call.

And in all life's up and downs,
when you set your eyes on Jesus,
He takes away all frowns.

If you're feeling down and really sad,
when you set your eyes on Jesus,
He will make you glad.

In life we're faced with many things,
but the answers to all problems He will bring—
when you set your eyes on Jesus.

SUDDENLY

Suddenly, in a moment of time, God turns it around;
And before you know, it a miracle is found.

Suddenly, in the blink of an eye,
There's all the joy replacing those sighs.

Suddenly, with God's favour, it's all change
And before you your life is rearranged.

Suddenly that promotion, or someone new—
All it takes is a God-like view.

Suddenly describes God's split-second ways
Of answering our prayers day after day.

Suddenly is the way we should expect.
When God moves in our lives we've no regrets.

Suddenly. His way. We faithfully wait.
But, one thing's for sure, he's never late.

Suddenly will come when we least expect.
If God has a list, suddenly next!

LOVE

HEALING LOVE

Hope comes riding on the wings of prayers,
floating upwards to the One who cares.

Our heavenly Father, loving to all,
hears your prayers and answers your call.

Sending angels just for you,
with gifts of faith to guide you through.

God-given faith will tear down walls,
healing all sickness when it comes to call.

No matter how bad things may appear to be
His healing love is all you need.

Take that love, don't let it go
and all your fears will melt like snow.

So trust and believe with all your heart,
and your sickness will depart.

THE SAVIOUR'S EYES

When I look into the Saviour's eyes,
I see a chasm of love, so deep and wide.

And if I were to step within,
I would fall head-over-heels in love with Him.

A healing love for all my tears
and forgiveness for all my years.

An overwhelming love that penetrates my soul,
even when my heart is cold.

The love in His eyes, always seeing,
searching deep into my inner being.

The love and abundance of His grace,
shine with radiance from His face.

A love that calls to peace and calm,
a reassuring love with open arms.

With no more cares and no more sighs,
such love, when you look into the Saviour's eyes.

MY FIRST LOVE

Where is that first love that I once knew,
with all those feelings and excitement
that I once had with you?

It all seems now so far away . . .
Yet it only seems like yesterday
that I couldn't wait to pray.

Meeting after meeting –
I just couldn't wait!
To be in your presence was absolutely great.

So much peace and joy that you gave,
If I could only find now
what once my heart would crave.

But if I think back on your words so true,
I can still hear your voice saying,
"I will never leave you."

So, knowing that you're still faithfully there,
I now feel your presence
and your loving care.

The excitement is back
and I'm refilled with yearning.
My first love is now returning!

ANOTHER DAY

Never ending ripples on the sea,
are God's love for you and me.

His voice is there on the waves,
Telling us all just what He gave.

But our ears are shut to His voice,
even though He gave us a choice.

"Choose life!" echoes across the waves of time.
Man replies, "Another day. We're just fine."

Tears of rain fall from above,
washing us in His heart-felt love.

What is God to do with Man,
But love us until we understand.

PEACE

THE PLACE BEYOND

The gentle wind blows so free,
across the land and out to sea.

If I could ride on the back of that wind,
it would take me to where true life begins.

A parallel time that does not bend.
A place where time never ends.

A place where there's no dark, only light,
where broken dreams are made alright.

Where words of timeless truth are found,
and rejoicing is an unending sound.

Love, peace and hope fill the air,
people singing and dancing everywhere.

And all things just so perfectly made—
everything new, with no decay.

Sparkling waters glisten like gems,
flowing peacefully without an end.

Scented flowers bow in the breeze,
as people worship on their knees.

From the Golden City where true life begins,
the Light of Life calls them in.

But until my time is called, I must carry on –
always dreaming of the place beyond . . .

OVER THE RAINBOW

When God's rainbow appears in the sky
It's a sign of His love for you and I.

Seven bows of colour, all blending together,
a covenant of His love, lasting forever.

Somewhere over the rainbow, there's a place waiting for you;
Where all troubles vanish, and dreams really come true.

Over the rainbow is a place of calm
where He waits with open arms.

We will one day soar high above
over the rainbow to a place of peace, joy and love.

SOAR HIGH AWAY

Spirit within, let's soar high away,
over the mountain tops to a brighter day.

Take me higher where together we can roam,
Reaching to that place that you call home.

Take me to where time doesn't cease.
Show me that place of heavenly peace.

Such joy, love and freedom so true—
I'm above life's troubles when I soar with you.

So impatiently I wait for another new day,
with you once again I can soar high away.

A GREAT DAY

Planning your future can be a daunting force.
When you give it to Jesus, He will set your course.

He knows what He's doing. He'll take care of things.
Great peace of mind to you He will bring.

His grace is sufficient for one day at a time.
When you hand it over to Jesus, all will be fine.

Give Him your life—He knows where to begin.
Just sit back and trust in Him.

So, when you wake up in the morning, just simply say:
"It's all yours, Jesus; I'm having a great day!"

ON GOD'S SHOULDERS

Up here on God's shoulders I am so tall,
free from all cares—free from them all.

Up here on God's shoulders He meets all my needs,
where dreams are met—the place to be.

Up here on God's shoulders all finance is met,
with no more striving and no more regret.

Up here on God's shoulders there're no more fears,
hearts are mended and no more tears.

Up here on God's shoulders there's no more pain.
Bodies are healed—like new again.

Up here on God's shoulders there's joy and peace,
an endless love that will never cease.

Up here on God's shoulders blessings are found.
Up here on God's shoulders—I'm never coming down.

HOPE

A BRAND NEW DAY

The moon and stars glitter all night,
with the Morning Star
shining so bright.

Night gives way to the morning dawn
and wakes the sun,
with his warming yawn.

Rays of warmth touch the ground.
It wakes up life,
with all its sounds.

Skies of blue and fields of green
and not a cloud
to spoil the scene.

The morning birds—merrily they sing
of God's new day,
of hope He brings.

And God, in his forgiving way,
gives us all
a brand new day.

TEARS OF ANGELS

Tears of angels raining down,
their tears like rivers flow
throughout the towns.

Tears of angels seeking the lost,
People not caring, at what cost!

Tears of laughter was once a sound,
Now only tears of sorrow can be found.

Tears of angels raining down,
Their tears like rivers flow
throughout the towns.

Tears of beauty that should have been,
now they're lost to tears of sin.

Tears of hope have come to replace
tears of despair on a doubting face.

Tears of joy fill the air!
The tears of angels . . .
. . . are no longer there.

RIGHTEOUS, THE HERO

The nations of the world are crying
and at the battlefront the lost, the fallen are dying.

The cry of the nations could be heard
across the heavens, "Send us a word!"

Then, from out of the ranks and all the tears,
came Righteous the Hero, with no fear.

His battle-cry is "Follow me!
I'll lead you on to victory!"

With the sound of his voice, all hope is born
And many gather at the sound of his horn.

But opposition and fear were amongst the crowd.
Their condemning voices grew so loud.

"He's not for us!" "Let us have our say!"
"Give us another!" "Let him die today!"

But death couldn't hold him, he had his say.
His word of salvation was here to stay.

From death to victory, Righteous the Hero rose.
And his story goes on, never to close.

OUTSIDE THE GATE

This new home of mine has a steel door,
a little bunk bed and not much more.

Life is so dark and full of despair.
The door is locked and nobody cares.

These four walls are my reward.
Confused, I thought I'd get applause.

In the other bunk I have a mate,
with tattooed hands that spell out 'hate'.

Having time to think of what went wrong,
seeking God for forgiveness, I ask to belong.

A dazzling hope enters like a deep flood,
a feeling inside of overwhelming love.

With peace of mind, and no desire to offend,
I have God's forgiveness and want to make amends.

A new life waits for me outside
of hope and a bright future in which to reside.

Not long now for me to wait
for the freedom that's outside the gate.

I've served my time, now a new life begins –
with God and me and, no longer, sin.

FAITH

WALKING ON GALILEE

He said, "Come! Trust me.
It's not hard—walking on Galilee."

If only I could!
But my mind asked if I should
walk on Galilee.

But there he was—standing there,
not afraid and without a care,
walking on Galilee.

With eyes fixed on him I gazed.
It was now or never to be brave,
walking on Galilee.

His arms outstretched is what I see,
saying, "Don't be afraid, come to me!"
walking on Galilee.

And now I am out of the boat,
not quite sure if I'll sink or float,
walking on Galilee.

He said, "Don't look down; look straight ahead.
There's nothing to fear; there's nothing to dread!"
walking on Galilee.

With faith and boldness, a step I take,
for I know all things possible he can make,
walking on Galilee.

For an instant I take my eyes off him.
I'm on my own! It's sink or swim!
walking on Galilee.

But all's not lost in the sea.
He reaches out and saves me!
walking on Galilee.

Back in the boat, all safe and sound,
I thank Jesus, who I found
walking on Galilee.

ALONG THE ROAD

He was in a world of darkness,
begging at the roadside.

His only hope was in passers by
but his feeble cries were denied.

Then he heard something new—
many steps instead of few.

His ears could hear the noise of the crowd:
cheers of excitement that were *so* loud!

He cried out, "Why the excitement? Why all the sound?"
The reply was: "Jesus, the healer, has come to town!"

Throwing away all fear and doubt,
blind Bartimaeus began to shout:

"Jesus, Jesus, heal my sight!"
Many rebuked him and said, "Be quiet!"

In desperation he shouted so loud
that Jesus heard it above the crowd.

Jesus stopped and said, "Call the man!"
They said, "On your feet!" and he began to stand.

Throwing his cloak away to the ground,
he made his way towards the sound.

Jesus asked, "What do you want of me?"
Blind Bartimaeus said, "Jesus, I want to see!"

Receiving his sight for the faith he showed,
Bartimaeus followed Jesus along the road.

GIVING

He said, "If you give to me your life will be free
from all life's poverty."

So when a giving heart starts to give,
abundance and prosperity start to live.

The more you give, the more comes back.
Receiving so much, there's no room for lack.

With opportunities to give, you pray for more.
Then no longer will want knock at your door.

If you give your time, money or love,
the flood gates of blessing will rain from above.

So remember: outgiving God—you'll never do,
because the more you try, the more He gives to you!

IF YOU ONLY BELIEVE

Who are you, Faith, that you should want of me?
I know only life and poverty.

I am Faith, the thing not seen.
I cross divides of broken dreams.

You speak, Faith, of thing I don't know,
leaving stirred up feelings inside to grow.

Tell me, Faith, if you are who you say,
why did you not come before today?

I, Faith, have been long in you.
You held me back, not ever used.

I am dead without action, dead as can be.
Without your words, I cannot be free.

I can save, I can heal, I can do anything you like.
I am always there, even through the night.

Once released by your words and from your heart,
There's nothing I can't do, once I start.

So speak your words, step out of the way.
And see if I don't do the things I say.

I am Faith, the size of a seed.
I'll even move mountains, if you only believe.

HUMOUR

THE DUDE

During the fourth watch of the night,
Jesus gave his Dudes a fright.

By walking upon the lake.
They cried out, "It's a ghost!"
Big mistake!

"Take courage, Dudes, don't be afraid.
It's me, your friend, I've come to save."

Peter Dude said, "Even though I shouldn't do,
tell me to come and I'll walk with you."

"Come, Dude," Jesus said.
"You can do it standing on your head."

Peter Dude, now out of the boat,
realized that he could float.

Towards Jesus, boldly he came,
all big-headed, awash with fame.

Making sure all the Dudes could see,
Peter Dude shouts, "Hey, Dudes, look at me!"

But then Peter Dude began to think . . .
Fear came and he began to sink.

Peter Dude cried, "I'm sinking in this sea!
Come quickly, Jesus, and save me!"

Jesus reached out and deftly caught him.
"Hey, Dude of little faith you didn't have to swim."

They both got into the boat.
Peter Dude, wet through, put on his coat.

And all the Dudes were raving
about Jesus' act of saving.

Left all the Dudes in a worshiping mood,
saying, "Truly he's the Son of the Great Dude!"

A GRIZZLY END

Daniel won King Darius's favour
and was known as his Number One Raver.

But the King's men didn't like what they saw
and set about inventing a new law.

Anyone caught praying to God or anything
would be thrown to the lions by order of the King.

Still Daniel, three times a day,
went down on his knees to pray.

And all the King's men put up a fuss
and reported him to King Darius.

King Darius, who was greatly distressed,
tried to rescue Daniel from this mess.

But actually the king had no choice
and called Daniel to hear his voice.

And King Darius, who was easily led,
was persuaded by his men, who said:

"Remember, O King, according to the law,
your decree must stand for evermore."

So the King gave the order and he was thrown in the den.
Said Darius to Daniel, "I hope this isn't your end!"

The King returned to his palace and couldn't sleep.
At first light he hurried to the den for a peep.

He called out hopefully, "Daniel, are you still fine?
Has your God rescued you from the mouth of the lions?"

"O King live forever! Those lions came and sat –
O King, they are no more than pussy cats!"

The King was so glad and took Daniel out of the den,
but the King's advisers came to a grizzly end!

ZACCHAEUS

Jesus entered Jericho and was passing through.
A man was there named Zacchaeus –
a chief tax collector
and wealthy too.

He wanted to see who Jesus was
and, being short, he could not see,
so he ran ahead and climbed up
into a sycamore tree.

When Jesus reached the spot
he looked up to say,
"Zacchaeus, come on down,
I must stay at your house today!"

All the people saw this
and began to mutter,
"He has gone to be the guest
of a sinner and a nutter."

But Zacchaeus was ready
to be held to account,
"If I've cheated anybody,
I'll pay back four times the amount!"

Jesus said, "Salvation has come to this house today.
This man, too, is a son of Abraham –
I came to seek and save."

THE NIGHTSHIFT WITH GOD

It's 3 o'clock in the morning . . .
woken from sleep, I'm yawning.

A voice says, "Write!"
"Not now, Lord, I'm tired—it's night!"

"Write!" echoes again in my head.
"But, Lord, I'm in bed!"

Under the covers, I'm safe and free.
"Write!" echoes again. He finds me.

I give up. As if I could win!
I find my pen and the writing begins.

Dawn breaks. I've finished his task,
not knowing if this is the last.

Who am I to question His untimely ways,
or His purpose, or what He says?

It's night again, hoping I'll sleep like a log,
but not yet knowing if I'll be on the nightshift with God . . .

CHOICE

TWO MORE DOORS

Two paths in life come our way—
one of hope, one of dismay.

At the start of the paths are two doors—
one of lack, one of more.

Both doors are open and voices within
say, "Enter and let us begin."

Which path is right? Which path is wrong?
If only I knew to whom I belong.

Along the path two more doors I see.
One says, 'Chained', one says, 'Free'.

Up ahead two more doors appear:
one of faith, one of fear.

An upward climb, I find myself go
to the top of life's hill, I see below.

In the distance of life, all I see
are two more doors waiting for me.

I reach the two doors that were ahead –
one of courage, one of dread.

How much further does this path take me?
If only I knew where it would lead.

Will this path never end?
With two more doors on a bend.

One of love, one of hate,
with a sign, 'Choose, before it's too late.'

Tired and weary with worn-out shoes,
two more doors: 'win' and 'lose'.

At last I see the end in sight,
two more doors: 'dark' and 'light'.

Above the light: salvation and a cross,
above the dark: damnation and loss.

I know I have to make a final choice,
and out of the light comes a voice.

"Walk this way and come right in.
This is where your life begins . . ."

Now, choose life . . . (Deut. 30 v.19)

THE LAKE

Born to swim in the lake of time,
some days with struggles and some days fine.

Tossing and turning against the waves,
sometimes fearful, sometimes brave.

Life's promise of hope—I keep on going,
but only broken dreams keep on showing.

And distant memories of times gone by,
rapidly fading to the sky.

Now tired and worn—not far to swim
and a wave of choice comes from Him.

"Choose life or death!" I hear Him say,
"The lake of time has one more day."

Now the distant shore comes into view.
Waiting there is the life I choose.

With family and friends all welcoming me,
a place of beauty and so much to see.

There's no more sadness and no more tears,
no more trouble and no more fears.

Only peace and joy and love to take,
and no more swimming the tiresome lake.

58

SAY YES

"Say yes."

"I am not ready yet to say yes to you.
I need more time to see this lifestyle through."
"Say yes."

"I am happy drinking and sometimes dancing,
with some passing acquaintances for romancing."
"Say yes."

"But all the above are part of my life.
It's far too much to sacrifice!"
"Say yes."

"I hear what you say, it's all very wrong.
I'll say yes later when it's all gone."
"Say yes."

"You say the two together just don't go.
Why I can't have both, I just don't know."
"Say yes."

"Lord, you're coming on strong, making me feel so bad,
and there's so much more I haven't had."
"Say yes."

"I know I can't win—you're not going away.
I'll sleep and we'll argue another day."
"Say yes."

As I lay my head down on the pillow to rest,
He has the last word:
"Say yes."

THE CORRIDOR OF LIFE

The corridor of life starts with joy,
and nothing else to do but play with toys.

With so many days and years still to pass,
the corridor of life seems to be so vast!

I've finally made it to the adulthood of life.
Whatever lies before me, I hope it's nice.

And then they tell me the best years have gone,
and all that's left ahead is an out-of-tune song!

In this corridor of life I have met them all:
the good, the bad, the wise and the fool.

So the corridor of life seems to hold no bars.
It welcomes all, with their troubles and their scars.

Now I approach the corridor's end.
Waiting for me is a wonderful friend.

"Welcome," says a reassuring voice.
"What's set before you is your choice."

Two more corridors ahead have been laid:
One leads to life, the other— the grave.

"I choose life!" I shout with glee.
The voice replies, "Then come follow me."

There's so much peace and no more strife.
When it's your time to choose,
choose the Corridor of Life!

JOURNEY'S END

A SEASON OF LIFE

At the end of their season the leaves fall from the trees,
making way for new life, a new life to conceive.

And so the season of life is for us to know,
We're born, we die, and it's the way we go.

But question; how did we live this given time?
Did we make our statement, or leave our mark behind?

On that last day when it's our time to leave,
Will there be many people there to grieve?

And when you stand before your maker and He sees
your life all through,
Will you hear the words, "Sorry I don't know you"?

Or will you hear "Well done my trusted friend,
A gift of eternal life is yours, a life that will never end"?

MAN

As man comes, so he departs
And what does he gain?
Since he toils for the wind,
ever chasing the same.

All mans efforts are for his mouth,
His appetite is never satisfied,
Ever consuming, nothing denied.

Whatever is has already been
And what will be has been before:
And God will call the past to account
When man knocks on heaven's door

A THANKFUL HEART

When I sit and ponder the things you've done,
even in times of trouble you turned them into fun.

Your grace, Lord, is sufficient in everything I do,
for without your timely help I could never get through.

And the closeness of your Spirit,
who's with me every day,
gives me great confidence in all I do and say.

You taught me well, Lord, to draw close to you,
and the rewards of your favour
just bless me through and through.

What more could I ask for when you're close to me,
but to be a witness for you that everyone can see.

So, Lord, I just carry on—doing my very best
until such time, Lord, you call me home to rest.

THE HELPING HAND

My first walk—I remember it well,
Holding Mother's hand in case I fell.

Tears of joy as she looked down on me,
The warmth of her love I could clearly see.

The time has come now, I'm away from home,
Able to walk all on my own.

And, chasing the wind, now I can run!
And chasing life with so much fun!

A new walk now is what I see,
With wife and child along side of me.

And life's pattern is full of repeats,
As my child finds his feet.

A tiny hand is holding mine.
My reassuring smile says all is fine.

And life's walk moves on again.
I find myself walking with a cane.

Unsure steps from a very old man,
And once again that helping hand.

A time to rest, a time to recap.
It's time to say, "It's my last nap."

My eyes are open and all I see
Is God's hand helping me.

HEAVEN ABOVE

The day started. It was just one more.
But the family, looking sad in black,
all go out the door.

Strange. Not so much as a goodbye.
Only yesterday they were all laughing
and on a high.

Was it something I did? Or something I said?
As far as I know all was fine
when I went to bed.

I busy myself, waiting for their return.
Then the door opens. Why do they all
have a look of concern?

I say, "Hello! Where have you been?"
Not even an answer—
just a morbid scene.

Silence fills the room with sadness.
It doesn't seem to leave.
Then I begin to wonder—can they not *see me?*

Again I speak and still they don't hear.
Now I know something's wrong.
I begin to fear.

66

I hear them talking about dear old me,
reminiscing about times that used to be.

With exasperation I begin to shout.
Not a blink of an eye!
My mind fills with doubt.

On the dresser I can see lots of cards,
with the words 'Sorry for your Loss',
some flowers in a vase.

My emotions run high,
my temper begins to grow.
Is there something going on that I don't know?

Then on my shoulder I feel a gentle hand,
and there behind me
is the form of a man.

He says his name is Jesus and all will be fine.
"Your time has come.
You must leave them behind."

With overwhelming joy and wrapped in his love,
I find myself leaving
for heaven above.

THE STRANGER

Thoughts of the old man sitting by the wayside
with memories of dreams that had long gone by.

But the contented smile on the old man's face
gave away the secret of that place . . .

It was there on the bench where he had had a chat
with a friendly stranger that came and sat.

The stranger spoke of a promised land of love
and that it was a gift from God above.

The stranger left and said, "I will come back."
Year after year, the old man returned to
the bench and sat.

He knew in his heart the stranger would come
and, somehow, the old man knew this day was the one.

The sun was shining, a soft breeze was blowing,
and all the cares of the world were now going.

The time was right—he had no more to say.
The old man knew this was his last day.

With a smile on his face and contented dim eyes,
he heard the stranger come and sit by his side.

The stranger, taking the old man's hand,
said, "Come, we're going home to that Promised Land."

WE'RE HOME

We soared hand-in-hand above the hills and out to sea,
Nothing holding me back, just my Angel and me.

Then above the clouds, higher and higher
from life below—
What was next I didn't know.

Up ahead was a glorious sight—a rainbow
of seven colours that I knew.
We stopped and stood on the arch
and God's creation came into view.

Through the rays of the sun, we wove in and out.
Tumbling over with joy, I began to shout.

My Angel just smiled with a look of love
As we carried on soaring higher above.

Now another sight was coming into view.
Though I'd never been there, it was a place that I knew.

My Angel spoke in a reassuring tone,
As he looked at me and said, "We're home."

THE JUDGEMENT

The page of life flicks on by,
faster and faster, like the blink of an eye.

A voice I hear from above,
"Show me a page that has love."

What about the old lady and the helping hand?
You remember, Lord, she said I was a nice man.

And what about the money in the poor man's hat?
Oh, you were there when I took it back?

Not that page, Lord, it's not very great.
I see what you mean, there was a lot of hate.

Oh yes, that time of extravagant greed.
But mine was greater than their need.

No, Lord, that day I got caught . . .
It wasn't me. It wasn't my fault.

Oh, the lying and the cheating?
Well, Lord, it came from the company I was keeping.

No more, Lord! What can be said?
I knew this day would come, a day of dread.

With regrets I try to make amends.
But, alas, the last page has been written, saying:
"The end."

LOST NOW FOUND

Lord Jesus, I believe you are God's Son,
That you came and died, for all the bad I've done.
Lord Jesus, forgive me for all my sinful ways.
Please come, Lord Jesus, into my life today.

www.ingramcontent.com/pod-product-compliance
Lightning Source LLC
Chambersburg PA
CBHW060657030426
42337CB00017B/2661